a PIZZA the size of the SUN

drawings by **JAMES STEVENSON**

poems by
JACK PRELUTSKY

a PIZZA
the size of
the SUN

SCHOLASTIC INC.
New York Toronto London Auckland Sydney

ISBN 0-590-37469-9

12   2/0

Printed in the U.S.A.   23

First Scholastic printing, September 1997

In memory of Marty Wallach

A Pizza the Size of the Sun

I'm making a pizza the size of the sun,
a pizza that's sure to weigh more than a ton,
a pizza too massive to pick up and toss,
a pizza resplendent with oceans of sauce.

I'm topping my pizza with mountains of cheese,
with acres of peppers, pimentos, and peas,
with mushrooms, tomatoes, and sausage galore,
with every last olive they had at the store.

My pizza is sure to be one of a kind,
my pizza will leave other pizzas behind,
my pizza will be a delectable treat
that all who love pizza are welcome to eat.

The oven is hot, I believe it will take
a year and a half for my pizza to bake.
I hardly can wait till my pizza is done,
my wonderful pizza the size of the sun.

Eyeballs for Sale!

Eyeballs for sale!
Fresh eyeballs for sale!
Delicious, nutritious,
not moldy or stale.
Eyeballs from manticores,
ogres, and elves,
fierce dragon eyeballs
that cook by themselves.

Eyeballs served cold!
Eyeballs served hot!
If you like eyeballs,
then this is the spot.
Ladle a glassful,
a bowlful, or pail—
Eyeballs! Fresh eyeballs!
Fresh eyeballs for sale!

My Elephant Is Different

My elephant is different
than most elephants I meet,
its ears are short and fuzzy,
it has feathers on its feet.
It's scaly like a lizard,
and it's furry like a skunk,
it sports a sort of auger
where there ought to be a trunk.

It doesn't much resemble
other elephants I find,
its tail is like a mushroom
on its tiny blue behind.
It cackles like a chicken,
and it's fourteen inches tall—
at times I think my elephant's
no elephant at all.

Spaghetti Seeds

"These are the best spaghetti seeds,"
the farmer promised me.
"And each of them will grow to be
a fine spaghetti tree."

I planted them a year ago . . .
that farmer is a phony.
I've not got one spaghetti tree—
just fields of macaroni.

News Brief

A defiant flock of pigeons
caused a minor episode
by obstructing local traffic
on a secondary road.

When the sheriff tried to move them,
they irreverently crowed,
so he radioed a tow truck
and had every pigeon towed.

A Frog, a Stick

A frog, a stick,
a shell, a stone,
a paper clip,
a chicken bone.
A feather quill,
a piece of string,
a ladybug,
a beetle wing.

A greenish wad
of bubble gum,
assorted keys,
and cookie crumbs.
A maple leaf,
a candy bar,
a rubber band,
a model car.

Potato chips
and soggy fries,
plus something
I can't recognize.
A broken watch,
a plastic cow . . .
that's what's inside
my pockets now.

My Brother Is a Doodler

My brother is a doodler,
he simply loves to scrawl,
he doodles, doodles, doodles
with his crayons on the wall.
He doodles on the windows,
and he doodles on the door,
then doodles, doodles, doodles
on the ceiling and the floor.

All day he doodles, doodles,
he doodles everywhere,
if there's no place to doodle,
he doodles in the air.
He doodles, doodles, doodles
on my pillow and my sheet,
and sometimes even doodles
on the bottoms of my feet.

The Puppy Made Off with My Slippers

The puppy made off with my slippers
and buried them both in the yard.
I now grow remarkable shoe trees—
it isn't especially hard.

I'm Wrestling with an Octopus

I'm wrestling with an octopus
and faring less than well,
one peek at my predicament
should be enough to tell.
It held me in a hammerlock,
then swept me off my feet,
I'm getting the impression
that I simply can't compete.

I'd hoped that I could hold my own,
but after just a while,
I ascertained I couldn't match
an octopus's style.
It flipped me by a shoulder,
and it latched onto a hip,
essentially that octopus
has got me in its grip.

I tried assorted armlocks,
but invariably missed,
and now I'm in a headlock,
and it's clinging to my wrist.
It's wound around my ankles,
and it's wrapped around my chest—
when grappling with an octopus,
I come out second best.

I Did a Nutty Somersault

I did a nutty somersault
and landed with a thump.
I struggled to my feet again
but tumbled on my rump.
I tried to keep my balance
but invariably fell,
and every time I toppled
I let out another yell.

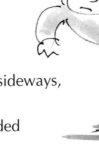

Backwards, forwards, even sideways,
I fell every sort of way,
as a growing crowd applauded
my theatrical display.
I flopped, I flipped, I skidded,
I performed a barrel roll.
My arms and legs kept flapping,
they were out of my control.

My feet shot out from under me
the moment I arose.
I took a flying header,
nearly damaging my nose.
So I suppose I'm qualified
to offer this advice—
when you try out *your* roller blades,
don't do it on the ice.

Oh Please Take Me Fishing!

"Oh please take me fishing, oh please, pretty please,"
insisted my sister the pest.
She drives me bananas when she's at her worst,
she bugs me when she's at her best.

She wouldn't give up, so I've got her along,
but I've not decided her fate.
Maybe I'll patiently teach her to fish—
maybe I'll use her for bait!

We Are Doddies

We are Doddies, smooth as eggs,
we've got bodies on our legs.
We've got heads with tiny brains,
we play leapfrog when it rains.

We are Doddies, often wet,
we don't know what we forget.
We are warmest when it's hot,
we are coldest when it's not.

We are Doddies, small and round,
we're not missing when we're found.
We are closest when we're near,
we're not there when we are here.

We are Doddies, we don't mind
if we leave ourselves behind.
So we never make a fuss,
we are Doddies, look for us.

The Children of the Moth

The children of the moth
are generally full.
They fill themselves with cloth,
it's generally wool.

They gnaw both night and day,
it seems they never sleep.
I wish they'd go away
and nibble on a sheep.

I WAS WALKING IN A CIRCLE WHEN I SPIED A PIECE OF PAPER COVERED WITH A PRETTY PICTURE COLORED YELLOW GREEN AND RED AS I PICKED IT UP I NOTICED THAT IT ALSO HAD SOME WRITING AND I KNEW THAT I SHOULD READ IT THIS IS WHAT THE WRITING SAID

A Pelican

A pelican uses its steam-shovel bill
to gather more fish than can possibly fill
its pelican belly.
It's not out of greed . . .
that bill is a trough where young pelicans feed.

The Parrots

The parrots, garbed in gaudy dress,
with almost nothing to express,
delight in spouting empty words . . .
they are extremely verbal birds.

Oblivious to all they say,
they often talk the day away.
At times they open up their beaks
and ramble on for weeks and weeks.

The parrots, when they voice a word,
are imitating what they've heard,
and yet they seem to love to chat—
do you know anyone like that?

I'm Practically Covered with Needles and Pins

I'm practically covered with needles and pins,
a teakettle's firmly affixed to my shins,
my ankles are clanking with clippers and keys,
and several spoons are attached to my knees.

The fork on my forehead is making me frown,
the bolts on my shoulders are weighing me down,
a jingle bell's ringing right under my nose,
and tacks add a finishing touch to my toes.

A hook is adhering to each of my ears,
my head is topped off by a mountain of gears,
my waist is encircled by washers and wheels,
and hinges are holding on fast to my heels.

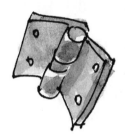

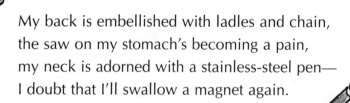

My back is embellished with ladles and chain,
the saw on my stomach's becoming a pain,
my neck is adorned with a stainless-steel pen—
I doubt that I'll swallow a magnet again.

Rollo

This is the saga of Rollo,
a fellow of average height.
Neither too plump nor too scrawny,
Rollo was just about right.

A steamroller rolled over Rollo,
changing him once and for all.
Now we admire him daily,
framed on our living room wall.

Backwards Forwards Silly Rhyme

I thguoht d'I etirw ekil siht yadot
esuaceb ti demees ekil nuf,
ev'I tog on rehto nosaer,
tub I ylerus t'nod deen eno.

tI ylbaborp sesufnoc uoy
eht tsrif emit taht uoy ees
eht sdrow lla nettirw sdrawkcab . . .
ti osla delzzup em.

tuB won ev'I nettog desu ot ti,
dna ylerus os evah uoy,
dna ev'I a llams noicipsus
taht uoy tsuj thgim yrt ti oot.

Miss Misinformation

I'm Miss Misinformation,
it's my gratifying task
to tell you all you need to know,
you only need to ask.
The seas are thick with elephants,
the skies are purple straw,
you measure with an octopus,
you hammer with a saw.

I'm filled with facts and figures
I gratuitously share.
The stars are silver footballs,
tangerines have curly hair.
Gorillas fly at midnight,
and a month has seven years,
tomatoes play the clarinet,
bananas have long ears.

I'm Miss Misinformation,
and there's nothing I don't know.
The moon is chocolate pudding,
macaroni grows in snow.
A buffalo is smaller
than the average bumblebee—
if you think of any questions,
simply bring them here to me.

When I Grow Up

When I grow up, I think that I
may pilot rockets through the sky,
grow orchards full of apple trees,
or find a way to cure disease.
Perhaps I'll run for president,
design a robot, or invent
unique computerized machines
or miniature submarines.

When I grow up, I'd like to be
the captain of a ship at sea,
an architect, a clown or cook,
the writer of a famous book.
I just might be the one to teach
a chimpanzee the art of speech . . .
but what I'll *really* be, I'll bet
I've not *begun* to think of yet.

Sardines

Their daily lives are bland,
and if they land—
they're canned.

Quentin Quimble Quamble Quayle

I'm Quentin Quimble Quamble Quayle,
an unrepentant tattletale,
repeating all I hear and see . . .
your secrets are not safe with me.
I recommend that you take care
of what you say when I am there.
Be cognizant of all you do,
I'm furtively observing you.

I'm Quentin Quimble Quamble Quayle,
I blab whenever I exhale,
on absolutely anyone . . .
it's how I choose to have my fun.
If I'm around, it surely means
that I will shortly spill the beans,
and anything you iterate
I'm certain to regurgitate.

My ears are keen, my ways are sly,
I sneak, I spy, I snoop, I pry.
You cannot trust me with a word,
I'll blurt out every word I've heard.
I even take it in my head
to broadcast things you *never* said,
embellishing with great detail . . .
I'm Quentin Quimble Quamble Quayle.

Today's a Foggy Foggy Day

Today's a foggy foggy day,
it's hard to see a thing,
I cannot see the robins,
though I think I hear them sing.
The flowers are invisible,
I can't discern the trees,
my feet are imperceptible,
I barely see my knees.

Today's a foggy foggy day,
it's dreary and it's weird,
the sun is not in evidence,
the sky has disappeared.
There's nothing I can recognize,
I'm feeling mystified,
and I suspect I'll find it's worse
as soon as I'm outside.

K. C. O'Fleer

I'm K. C. O'Fleer,
famous train engineer,
at railroading I am supreme.
I'm on the express
known as Anyone's Guess,
and we've got a full head of steam.

I'm K. C. O'Fleer,
we are still sitting here,
I doubt that we'll go anywhere.
We're loaded with coal,
but the train cannot roll—
the wheels are all perfectly square.

My Gerbil Seemed Bedraggled

My gerbil seemed bedraggled,
I believed that it was blue,
so I got it a companion . . .
now I had exactly two.
They got along together,
but it still was a surprise
when one morning I detected
seven pairs of gerbil eyes.

Then I had a dozen gerbils,
and another dozen more,
every day I had more gerbils
than I'd had the day before.
Soon I had a hundred gerbils,
double, triple that amount,
as the population blossomed,
and I started losing count.

There are gerbils on the bookshelves,
in the kitchen, on the stairs,
bowls and baskets full of gerbils
on the tables and the chairs.
There are gerbils in the corners,
gerbils all along the floors,
gerbils searching through the closets
and exploring all the drawers.

It's a gerbil inundation,
they take every inch of space,
when I waken in the morning,
gerbils gaze into my face.
I am overrun by gerbils,
gerbils, gerbils everywhere,
so I hope you'd like a gerbil—
I've got lots of them to spare!

I Made a Perpetual Motion Machine

I made a perpetual motion machine,
the only one anyone ever has seen.
I put it together without any plan,
and so I was more than surprised when it ran.

I made it of skateboards and bicycle parts,
discarded pianos and old shopping carts.
I didn't write down how I did what I did,
I don't even know how I put on the lid.

Its power apparently hasn't a source,
not gas or electric, atomic or horse.
Yet somehow it's run unabated for years,
without any wear on the pistons or gears.

I've recently wished my amazing device
would shut itself down and not be so precise.
It's all on account of an unforeseen turn
that finds me expressing increasing concern.

I freely confess I'm not having much fun,
I'm sleeping too fast, and I eat on the run.
I slipped and fell in while attempting to clean
my perfect perpetual motion machine.

Penguins

Penguins cautiously reside
on our planet's underside,
where they're careful not to cough,
lest they trip and tumble off.

I'm Usually a Speedy Horse

I'm usually a speedy horse,
today I'm very slow.
I'm hardly making headway
as along the road I go.

I'm slower than a tortoise
or a sloth atop a tree—
my rider has decided
that he ought to carry me.

An Extraterrestrial Alien

An extraterrestrial alien
I never expected to meet
is bouncing about in my bedroom
on half of its forty-four feet.
It made its appearance this morning,
when, plummeting out of the sky
without a protective enclosure,
it landed, undamaged, nearby.

It didn't resemble a rocket,
it certainly wasn't a bird,
yet no one but me seemed to notice
that anything odd had occurred.
I couldn't contain my excitement
and raced there uncommonly fast.
"Delighted to see you!" it burbled,
then laughed as I panted, aghast.

That extraterrestrial alien
displayed unmistakable charm,
it bowed at the waist, then embraced me
with half of its forty-four arms.
It danced with apparent abandon,
I stared in unblinking surprise,
enthralled by the twenty-two twinkles
in half of its forty-four eyes.

"I'm glad that you like me!" it gurgled.
"You wish to be friends, I presume?"
"I do!" I replied, and decided
to hide it inside of my room.
That extraterrestrial alien
I never expected to find
informs me it's coming to dinner—
I hope that my parents don't mind.

The Jellybean Brigade

They came to town, they came to town,
the Jellybean Brigade.
They marched about in bright array,
a rainbow on parade.

They swaggered in the broiling sun,
instead of in the shade.
They're nothing but a puddle now—
the Jellybean Brigade.

I Put the Cat Out

I put the cat out and I let the dog in,
the cat ran away and the dog licked my chin.
I let the cat in and I put the dog out,
the dog ambled off and the cat lay about.

The dog soon returned, I allowed it inside,
it dashed at the cat, who attempted to hide.
Inside and outside and this way and that,
it's tricky to balance a dog and a cat.

Gloppe's Soup Shoppe

I am Gladiola Gloppe,
I cook soups at *GLOPPE'S SOUP SHOPPE*,
every one of which is certain to delight.
I prepare for you each day
an astonishing array,
here are samples to entice your appetite:

SALAMANDER SALMON SLUG

BAT BEGONIA BARLEY BUG

RUTABAGA BACON BARRACUDA BRAN

ANACONDA GREEN SARDINE

TURTLE TURKEY TANGERINE

BEETLE BEAN BANANA FROG FALAFEL FLAN

HIPPO HIP HYENA HAIR

CREAM OF CAMEL CAMEMBERT

GOPHER GUMBO GOAT GORILLA GOOBER GOOSE

PUFFIN PORK PIRANHA PEAS

COTTON CANDY COTTAGE CHEESE

MASHED MOSQUITO MARINARA MANGO MOOSE

GINGER GERBIL JONQUIL JAM

CURRY COLA CACTUS CLAM

CALAMARI CORN KOALA KEROSENE

RUMP OF RHINO RAISIN RYE

DIESEL DUMPLING DRAGONFLY

WEASEL WIENER WEEPING WILLOW WOLVERINE

If you happen to stop by,
won't you give my soups a try?
You'll discover you will savor every drop.
The aromas are unique,
and the flavors last a week . . .
you'll just love what I concoct at *GLOPPE'S SOUP SHOPPE!*

A Knothead

To come out and call you a knothead
would not be a nice thing to do.
However, I can't help but notice
that woodpecker landing on you.

An Unobservant Porcupine

An unobservant porcupine
backed up into its brother.
Since then they've been inseparable—
they're stuck on one another.

I Am Your Mirror Image

I am your mirror image,
and everything I do
is an exact reflection
of all that's done by you.
I only move when you do,
when you are still, I stop.
You skip, I'm sure to skip along,
you hop, I also hop.

I'm with you like your shadow,
I'm agile, swift, and deft.
You gesture with your right hand,
I match you with my left.
I laugh when you are happy,
when you are sad, I cry,
and if you blink an eye at me,
a blink is my reply.

I am your mirror image,
I'm present when you're here.
The moment you are absent,
I'm sure to disappear.
I count on your existence
and live your life reversed . . .
I never do a single thing
unless you do it first.

Hurry Grandma Hurry

Hurry Grandma hurry,
Grandma look at me,
I'm right side up, I'm upside down,
I'm swinging from a tree.
I'm jumping like a squirrel,
I think that I can fly—
Grandma please don't worry,
Grandma please don't cry.

Hurry Grandma hurry,
see what I can do,
I'm roller-skating backwards
across the avenue.
Here's a luscious little bug,
I think I'll take a bite—
Grandma stop your screaming,
everything's all right.

Hurry Grandma hurry,
Grandma watch me please,
I'm climbing up a ladder,
I'm dangling by my knees.
I found this giant spider
that was stuck in globs of paint,
Grandma take a closer look—
whatever made you faint?

I Think My Computer Is Crazy

I think my computer is crazy,
it's gone off its rocker today,
the screen is impossibly scrambled,
and I can't control the display.
Illegible symbols are flashing
in places they just don't belong,
it's surely no help with my homework,
every last answer is wrong.

I'd always depended upon it,
but now its behavior has changed,
it's churning out absolute drivel,
it's clear my computer's deranged.
It's making disheartening noises,
like kangaroos hopping on fruit,
it thoroughly garbles my input,
then burbles, **"THIS DOES NOT COMPUTE!"**

Something inside my computer
is buzzing like billions of bees,
even my mouse is affected,
it seems to be begging for cheese.
I guess I know why my computer
is addled and may not survive—
my brother inserted bologna
into the floppy disk drive.

I Made Something Strange with My Chemistry Set

I made something strange with my chemistry set,
something all gluey and blue,
something a little like half-scrambled eggs,
mingled with vegetable stew.
As soon as I'd made it, it started to move,
it slid from my bench to the floor.
I knew where it was without having to look,
its odor was hard to ignore.

It bubbled and sloshed as it oozed through my room,
then started ingesting my toys.
It seemed to enfold them and slurp them away,
while making a blubbery noise.
That slobbery thing had a will of its own,
it snuffled all over the house,
it frightened my sister and panicked the cat
and melted my mother's best blouse.

It soon found the kitchen, and after the bread,
the butter and cheese disappeared.
It slopped up the oleomargarine too,
and now it's grown even more weird.
I'd better undo it before it decides
to try something totally vile.
Right now it's en route to my kid brother's room—
I guess I can wait just a while.

A Triangular Tale

I
DO
NOT
KNOW
AT ALL HOW
I GOT STUCK
INSIDE THIS PIECE
OF PIE AND I'M
UNSURE HOW TO
BEGIN TO GET OUT
OF THE FIX I'M IN. THIS
TRIANGLE IS SIMPLY NOT
AN ENTERTAINING SORT
OF SPOT SO I CAN SAY WITHOUT
A DOUBT I'D LIKE TO LEAVE AND **WOW**. . . .

I'm out!

The Manatee

I'm partial to the manatee,
which emanates no vanity.
It swims amidst anemones
and hasn't any enemies.

Bugs! Bugs!

B ugs! Bugs!
I love bugs,
yes I truly do,
great big pink ones,
little green stink ones,
yellow bugs and blue.
I put you in my pockets,
and I wear you in my hair.
You are my close companions,
I take you everywhere.

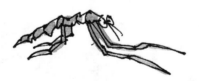

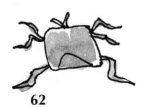

Bugs! Bugs!
I love bugs,
any shape or size,
thin ones, fat ones,
long ones, flat ones,
bugs with bulging eyes.
I hug you and I kiss you
and I bounce you on my knee.
No matter what I'm doing,
my bugs are close to me.

Bugs! Bugs!
I love bugs,
bugs you are my friends,
square ones, round ones,
half a pound ones,
bugs with big rear ends.
I love to watch you scamper,
and I love to watch you chew.
I've got no doubt about it—
bugs, I'm bugs for you!

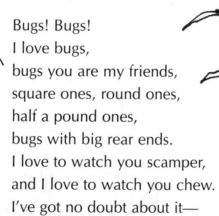

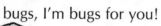

Mister Pfister Gristletwist

I'm Mister Pfister Gristletwist,
preeminent contortionist,
exhibiting for all to see
my peerless elasticity.
Quadruple-jointed, more or less,
I flex into a letter S,
then stretch a little extra, and
convolve into an ampersand.

I further curve and concentrate
to turn into a figure **8**.
From there it's not too far to go
to tie myself into a bow.
I fold myself in half, and then
refold myself in half again,
and next, to gasps and accolades,
arrange my arms and legs in braids.

I'm certainly a striking sight
when I'm a bowline on a bight,
or when I writhe into a box
too tiny for a pair of socks.
Alack! I'm in an awkward spot.
I've got my body in a knot
that even *I* can't budge a bit—
I hope that I get used to it!

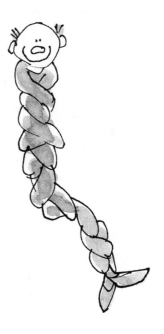

The Manners of the Moopies

The manners of the Moopies
tend to be unorthodox . . .
they put pudding in their pockets,
they stuff oatmeal in their socks.
They recline on mashed potatoes,
they tie wieners to their ears,
they smear jelly on their noses
as they swing from chandeliers.

Some people think the Moopies
are a boorish little group
when they roll in squashed bananas,
when they wash with lentil soup.
But *I* believe the Moopies
are a fascinating bunch,
and whenever I am able,
I invite them out to lunch.

Do Not Approach an Emu

Do not approach an emu,
the bird does not esteem you.
It wields a quick and wicked kick
that's guaranteed to cream you.

I Sailed on Half a Ship

I sailed on half a ship
on half the seven seas,
propelled by half a sail
that blew in half a breeze.
I climbed up half a mast
and sighted half a whale
that rose on half a mighty wave
and flourished half a tail.

Each day, with half a hook
and half a rod and reel,
I landed half a fish
that served as half a meal.
I ate off half a plate,
I drank from half a glass,
then mopped up half the starboard deck
and polished half the brass.

When half a year had passed,
as told by half a clock,
I entered half a port
and berthed at half a dock.
Since half my aunts were there
and half my uncles too,
I told them half this half-baked tale
that's half entirely true.

The Improbable Emporium

THE IMPROBABLE EMPORIUM

is open every day,
filled with everything that anyone could need.
There's a saddle for your sea horse
in an aqueous display,
sets of sandals styled to suit your centipede.

There are lights that make things darker,
graceful kites designed of stone,
a container that can catch an evening breeze.
There's a knife for slicing water
and a leather saxophone,
there's a sofa made entirely out of cheese.

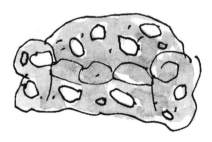

There are ottomans for otters,
special piccolos for pigs,
tubes of oil to stop the loudest mouse's squeak,
coils of dental floss for hippos,
finely crafted eagle wigs,
tiny barbells to improve your frog's physique.

If you'd like a fur umbrella
with a built-in cuckoo clock,
or perhaps a new invisible beret,

THE IMPROBABLE EMPORIUM

has both of them in stock,
and remember, they are open every day.

My Fish Was Small

My fish was small,
my fish was gold,
but now my fish
is still and cold.

My fish no more
will splash and splish.
My fish is gone

I flush my fish.

My Mother Makes Me Chicken

My mother makes me chicken,
her chicken makes me cough.
I wish that when she made it,
she took the feathers off.

"I'm Ceiling Fad!" A Money Boned

"I'm ceiling fad!" a money boned.
"Alas!" a carrot pride.
"I'm wheeling feared!" a cork stalled out.
"I'm fine!" a loafer guide.
The mammals coned, the ribbons gasped,
the slats declined to beep,
the sows were truly column,
and the woes prepared to creep.

The mats and rice could meet no eels,
the bleep refused to sheet,
the meals were sad, the wishers find,
the forces stamped their heat.
A wizard leapt in sorrow.
"I am hired!" clucked a ten.
The hacks would not stop yowling.
"Oh how roomy!" wept a glen.

The mugs began to butter,
and the shares began to bake,
the hogs announced, "We're freckled!"
"I'm snuffled!" hissed a rake.
"It's roaring!" chirped the bobbins,
and the blinks agreed, "It's manned!"
A box was clearly fathered,
and the stinks could hardly land.

A measle warned, a fever bust,
as wigs appeared to pail.
The soles were mad, the merits phoned.
"I quiver!" said a shale.
The terms decided not to walk,
the barrows shut their speaks,
and all because it pained and roared
for watts of soggy leaks.

Dan the Invisible Man

I'm Dan the invisible man,
so don't bother looking for me.
No matter how watchful you are,
I'm someone you simply can't see.
Although I eat visible food,
I still remain perfectly clear,
and if I stopped talking to you,
you'd have no idea I was here.

I love to relax in the tub
and scrub my invisible skin,
then comb my invisible hair
and shave my invisible chin.
I wear an invisible shirt,
invisible trousers and vest.
I really don't know why I do,
you can't even tell that I'm dressed.

I flash an invisible smile,
I strike an invisible pose,
I scratch my invisible ears,
I blow my invisible nose.
I recently went to the beach
and got a spectacular tan.
Of course I can't prove it, because
I'm Dan the invisible man.

My Brother's Really Stingy

My brother's really stingy,
he's the lowest, he's the worst.
He never shares his lollipops
unless he licks them first.

Someone Swiped the Cookies

Someone swiped the cookies
that were really meant for me.
I'm sure I know who did it,
she'll regret her little spree.
She snuck into the pantry
where she found the cookie jar,
she thinks she's really clever,
but she won't get very far.

I'm tracking down the culprit,
she should not be hard to find.
She left a very messy trail
of cookie crumbs behind.
There she is! I've got her!
She has crumbs around her lips!
Oh no! She finished every one . . .
my luscious chocolate chips.

I'm Wearing an Enchanted Hat

I'm wearing an enchanted hat
upon my lovely locks.
I made it from a pillowcase,
bandannas, rags, and socks.
I painted it more colors
than I've even learned to name.
The size and shape keep changing,
though the colors stay the same.

No sooner did I wear it
than it was apparent that
my remarkable creation
was no ordinary hat.
I happened to be thinking
of my missing teddy bear,
when suddenly atop my head,
I felt it sitting there.

When I have got my hat on,
all I need to do is wish.
If I wish for chocolate pudding,
it appears upon a dish.
I have wished for giant crayons
and a dancing kangaroo,
a miniature unicorn,
and each of them came true.

No matter what I wish for,
it is granted instantly.
If it can fit inside my hat,
it simply comes to be.
I'm learning what to never
ever wish for anymore—
I get tired of escaping
from my tiny dinosaur.

Lester

Every evening, right at eight,
Lester starts to levitate.
Rising from his easy chair,
Lester hovers in the air.
Lester doesn't show surprise
at his unsupported rise,
noting, as the ceiling nears,
"It's been going on for years!"

Lester seems a trifle smug,
four full feet above the rug,
obviously pleased that he
breaks the laws of gravity.
Puffed with self-important pride,
Lester says, "I'm mystified,
but it's eminently clear
I alone can dangle here!"

No one, Lester least of all,
knows why Lester doesn't fall.
Still, one can't deny the fact
that he stays aloft, intact.
After two full hours have passed,
Lester whines, "I'm sinking fast!"
Every evening, right at ten,
Lester settles down again.

I Met a Dozen Duhduhs

I met a dozen Duhduhs
in my neighborhood one day,
and though I tried to talk to them,
"DUHDUH!" was all they'd say.
"Excuse me, do you have the time?"
I asked them cordially.
They seemed to be befuddled,
and said **"DUHDUH!"** back to me.

"You think it looks like rain?" I said,
and pointed at the sky.
They didn't bother looking up,
"DUHDUH!" was their reply.
I tried again and asked their names,
they didn't seem to care.
They muttered **"DUHDUH! DUHDUH!"**
just as if I weren't there.

They respond to every question
with their dopey Duhduh grunts.
They say **"DUHDUH!"** to each other,
sometimes even all at once.
Snorting **"DUHDUH! DUHDUH! DUHDUH!"**
is the only thing they do,
so I'm glad I'm not a Duhduh,
and I hope you're not one too.

Opossums

Opossums at times take a notion to drop
whatever they're doing and come to a stop.
It's called "playing possum," and clearly it's why
they're mostly ignored by the folks passing by.

When they're playing possum, opossums don't stir,
they don't move a muscle or ruffle their fur.
Upon these occasions opossums are prone
to lie on the ground and resemble a stone.

When they're playing possum, opossums don't sense
the comings and goings of current events.
Their energy's focused on trying to strive
to make you believe that they aren't alive.

When they're playing possum, opossums appear
to be unaware that there's anyone near.
They never revive till you're well on your way—
when they're playing possum, opossums don't play.

I Am Riding on a Cloud

I am riding on a cloud
in the middle of the sky,
making idle conversation
with the birds who happen by.
I'm uncertain how I got here,
but I surely do not care.
I'm enchanted to be floating
unencumbered in the air.

I may try to catch a rainbow
with my rainbow-catching mitt,
build imaginary castles,
or do nothing else but sit.
What I do is unimportant,
just as long as I can stay
in my chariot of billows
on this dreamy summer day.

Paula Prue, I'm Mad at You

Paula Prue, I'm mad at you,
I don't like the things you do.
You dropped ice cream down my shirt,
that's no place for your dessert.

Paula Prue, I'll pay you back
when I launch my sneak attack.
Some day soon I'll get my chance—
you'll have pizza down your pants.

Herman Sherman Thurman

I'm Herman Sherman Thurman,
and I'm perfect . . . that's a fact.
No matter the activity,
I'm thorough and exact.
I waken every morning
at eleven after eight,
not half a second sooner
nor a quarter second late.

I measure out my cereal—
three hundred puffs of rice,
plus thirty-seven raisins,
one has got to be precise.
My manners are fastidious,
I'm groomed impeccably.
I'm positively flawless
as you'll doubtlessly agree.

I'm Herman Sherman Thurman.
You'll invariably find
that my teeth are brightly gleaming,
and my shoes are highly shined.
My trousers are immaculate,
my shirt and tie are clean.
Some people say I'm tedious—
I wonder what they mean.

Dixxer's Excellent Elixir

Dexter Dixxer mixed elixir
in his quick elixir mixer.
"It's an excellent elixir,"
Dexter boasted, "very fine
for afflictions which assail you,
aches which irritate and ail you,
guaranteed to rarely fail you,
only nineteen ninety-nine!"

His elixir tasted icky,
it was fishy, squishy, sticky,
just to swallow it was tricky,
and I tried to spit it out.
But too late! My tongue already
started turning to spaghetti,
and my hair was red confetti
with a touch of sauerkraut.

I grew feathers on my belly,
all my fingers felt like jelly,
then my feet got really smelly,
and my ears were green as limes.
I was squawking, I was squealing,
and I had a sinking feeling,
so I jumped up to the ceiling,
and I sneezed eleven times.

I was yipping, I was yapping,
as my kneecaps started clapping,
then my earlobes started flapping,
and my nose turned violet.
So I ran and told my mother,
"This elixir's like no other!"
Now I share it with my brother—
it's the best elixir yet!

Llook!

Llook at all the llovely llamas,
llama papas, llama mamas,
llively lleaping llittle llamas—
llots of llama panoramas!

Please Remove Seal

PLEASE REMOVE SEAL BEFORE USING THIS PRODUCT,
the sign on the box clearly read.
I don't have a seal, but I'm taking no chances—
I'll toss out my walrus instead.

I Do Not Like the Sunshine

I do not like the sunshine,
I'm dampened by the rain,
I think that clouds are ugly,
and snowflakes are a pain.
The stars are unattractive,
I shudder at the moon,
I'm burdened by a butterfly,
I blanch at a balloon.

Bananas are annoying,
I fail to stomach cheese,
I disapprove of flowers,
I tolerate no trees.
Tomatoes are vexatious,
I'm pestered by a plum,
I find a frog offensive,
gorillas make me glum.

I loathe a chair and table,
a sofa makes me sore,
a window's clearly silly,
I'm put out by a door.
I countenance no mountain,
I'm sickened by the sea,
and I don't care the slightest
if you don't care for me.

Eureka!

Eureka! At last I've succeeded,
my experiment's finally done.
I've made an incredible creature,
the only one under the sun.

There's never been anything like it,
part puppy, part kitten, part mouse—
and now I must learn how to stop it
from chasing itself through the house.

A Teenage Hippopotamus

A teenage hippopotamus
is living overhead.
I hear him every morning
when he bumbles out of bed.
He crashes through his living room
and makes my ceiling shake.
A teenage hippopotamus
is very hard to take.

That teenage hippopotamus
is louder than a train.
He loves to blast his radio,
it's driving me insane.
He keeps it on around the clock,
it blares and blares and blares—
I'm moving to the place next door,
where lions live upstairs.

I'm Happy as Anyone Ever Could Be

I'm happy as anyone ever could be,
there's no one on earth half as happy as me,
for I just found out at the doctor's today
I'm *really* allergic to liver . . . HOORAY!

Oh Mother, I Am Blue Today

"Oh Mother, I am blue today,
I don't know why or how.
There's never been another child
as blue as I am now."

"I see you're blue," my mother said,
"and this is what I think—
if you would rather not be blue,
don't bathe again in ink."

Swami Gourami

I'm Swami Gourami,
my powers are vast,
I've mastered the craft
of predicting the past.
I need but a second's
reflection to know
exactly what happened
a second ago.

I'm Swami Gourami,
I daily amaze,
revealing old minutes
and hours and days.
My vision is eerie,
uncanny, unique,
I'm able to gaze
at the previous week.

The future's too easy
for me to depict,
I dwell on the past,
which is hard to predict.
Last month is apparent,
no less than last year,
and long-ago decades
are perfectly clear.

I'm Swami Gourami,
I'm one of a kind,
unlocking the past
with my mystical mind.
My brain is stupendous,
supernal, sublime—
what's more, I'm correct
nearly half of the time.

Whopper!

I am sitting in the middle
of a whopper of a whale,
where there's scant illumination,
and the air is still and stale.
My monotonous enclosure
is predominantly gray,
and is surely no location
I would choose to spend my day.

There is no one to converse with
in a whale's digestive tract.
I am bored with my surroundings,
and I wish that I had packed.
Without any sort of warning
I was eaten like a bean.
Now I'm stranded in the center
of a living submarine.

I see no way of escaping,
so I'm throwing up my hands,
and unless I'm extricated,
I'm not making any plans.
I'd appreciate suggestions,
simply drop them in the mail.
Just address them to the belly
of this whopper of a whale.

I'm All Mixed Up

I'm AlL mIxED uP,
i'M aLl MiXed Up,
I dON't KnoW whAT tO Do.
I dO NOt thINK i'M me tODAy,
i WoNdeR iF I'M YoU.
mY voICE is nOt My VOice TOday,
it sOUnDS enTIrELY wrONg,
and mANY ThOugHts iNsIDe mY hEaD
i'm CeRTaIN dON'T bElOng.

106

My eYes aRE nOT My eYES toDaY,
mY nOse Is NOt MY nOSE,
my shOES aRE UNfAmiliaR,
I dOn'T REcOgnIZE mY cLOTheS.
My EaRs ArE NoT mY eArs tODay,
mY Hair iS nOt MY hAir,
I eVen thiNk i'M WeAriNg
soMeOnE elSe'S uNdERwEar.

NO mATter wHAt i writE ToDAy,
IT COMes oUt LOOking sTraNgE.
I HOpE ThaT i Can FIGurE ouT
a WaY TO maKE iT ChanGe.
i'M lOokinG cLOsELy at This pOEm,
bUT STilL dOn'T HAvE a CLue—
i'M ALL miXed Up,
I'M alL MIxED uP,
i Don'T KNOw WHat To dO.

I Got out of Bed

I got out of bed,
sensing something was strange,
and swiftly discerned
that I'd gone through a change.
My smile in the mirror
reflected a frown,
the head on my shoulders
had turned upside-down.

The mirror revealed
that I wasn't quite me,
my eyes filled the space
where my lips used to be.
My upside-down ears
seemed unwieldy and weird,
and the hair on my head
had the look of a beard.

If I should go out
in the rain, I suppose
that water would fill
my unfortunate nose.
The only advantage
I find in my head,
it's taught me one lesson—
don't get out of bed!

There Are Zebras on the Ceiling

There are zebras on the ceiling
dancing upside-down ballet.
A giraffe is in the foyer,
and it will not go away.
There's a chicken in the kitchen
playing checkers with a quail,
and a turtle's running races
with a very speedy snail.

My father's growing feathers,
and my mother's ten feet tall.
A weasel and a wallaby
are whistling on the wall.
The cheese has turned to butter,
and the butter's turned to bread.
The tub is full of buzzards,
and a bear is in my bed.

The furniture is shrinking,
and the den has disappeared.
My sister's sprouting antlers,
and the puppy has a beard.
A marmoset is marching
with a mallard and a mouse.
It's another normal Monday—
I just *love* it at our house!

I Often Repeat Repeat Myself

I often repeat repeat myself,
I often repeat repeat.
I don't I don't know why know why,
I simply know that I I I
am am inclined to say to say
a lot a lot this way this way—
I often repeat repeat myself,
I often repeat repeat.

I often repeat repeat myself,
I often repeat repeat.
My mom my mom gets mad gets mad,
it irritates my dad my dad,
it drives them up a tree tree tree,
that's what they tell they tell me me—
I often repeat repeat myself,
I often repeat repeat.

I often repeat repeat myself,
I often repeat repeat.
It gets me in a jam a jam,
but that's the way I am I am,
in fact I think it's neat it's neat
to to to to repeat repeat—
I often repeat repeat myself,
I often repeat repeat.

Milk!

I only had known it in cartons
my parents picked up at the store.
I recently saw where it comes from—
I do not drink milk anymore!

Chipmunk, Chipmunk

Chipmunk, chipmunk, just like that,
hopped into the pudding vat.

Chipmunk, chipmunk, take a bow—
you're a chocolate chipmunk now!

I'm Drifting Through Negative Space

I'm drifting through negative space,
a frown on my lack of a face,
attempting to hear
with a tenuous ear
what nobody says in this place.
Undressed in unknowable clothes,
I strike an impossible pose,
then rest my non-head
on my shadowy bed,
and when I awaken, I doze.

I'm eating a make-believe bite,
today in the negative night.
The water I drink
from my fictional sink
is dry as the darkness is light.
I toss an ephemeral ball
against an impalpable wall.
It bounces and lands
in my vanishing hands—
it's hard to keep track of it all.

I'd like to be positive, but
I'm stuck in a negative rut.
I laugh when I'm sad,
when I'm angry, I'm glad,
whatever I open, I shut.
I'm running an opposite race,
maintaining an imprecise pace.
I lose when I win,
going out coming in—
it's eerie in negative space.

A Fine Head of Lettuce

I'm a fine head of lettuce,
a handsome romaine.
I haven't a cranium
made for a brain.

I'm simple and shy,
I remain on my own.
I'm known in the garden
as lettuce alone.

An Unsavory Tomato

An unsavory tomato
felt disgruntled, glum, and cross,
having just been judged substandard
for a salad, soup, or sauce.

With unmitigated rancor
it declaimed, "I've been disgraced!"
In unbridled agitation
that irate tomato paced.

Frenetica Fluntz

Hello everyone, I'm Frenetica Fluntz,
I do many things, and I do them at once.
This makes me extremely amazing to see,
it also saves time, as I'm sure you'll agree.

I sleep as I eat and I eat as I drink
and I drink as I shout and I shout as I think
and I think as I draw and I draw as I walk
and I walk as I read and I read as I talk
and I talk as I laugh and I laugh as I sing
and I sing as I slide and I slide as I swing
and I swing as I run and I run as I hop
and I hop as I dust and I dust as I mop
and I mop as I skate and I skate as I sweep
and I sweep as I write and I write as I sleep.

There's nobody else who can manage such stunts . . .
I'm one of a kind, I'm Frenetica Fluntz.

I Do Not Wish to Go to School

"I do not wish to go to school,"
  insisted Sarah Sue,
"and Mother, if you make me,
  I will eat a worm or two."

"Do you mean worms like these, my dear?"
  her mother firmly said.
"I got them in the garden,
  they're extremely long and red.

"They're both the very juiciest
  and plumpest I could find."
"I'm off for school," said Sarah Sue,
  "for I have changed my mind!"

I'd Never Need a Haircut

I'd never need a haircut
if I didn't have a head,
and probably could manage
with no pillows on my bed.
I'd toss away the woolen cap
that shields me from the snow,
and soon dispense with tissues,
for I'd have no nose to blow.

I wouldn't need a toothpick,
for I'd have no teeth to pick.
I'd have no tongue to talk with,
and I'd have no lips to lick.
I could slice a million onions
without shedding any tears,
and never have to wash behind
my nonexistent ears.

I'd have a new perspective
if my head should disappear,
and find it quite a challenge
showing anger, joy, or fear.
My parents would be puzzled,
they'd be baffled, they would stare,
when they made the observation
that my noodle wasn't there.

There might be minor drawbacks
if the space above my neck
should become the site of nothing
more substantial than a speck.
I'd have to make adjustments
when I wanted to be fed—
I'd have a different outlook
if I didn't have a head.

It's Hard to Be an Elephant

It's hard to be an elephant,
enormous, broad, and tall.
I can't attend the cinema,
the seats are all too small.
It's practically impossible
for me to board a bus,
the tires often flatten,
and the driver makes a fuss.

I'm ushered out of luncheonettes,
the waitresses are rude.
They fume, "We cannot feed you,
for you'll finish all our food."
I'm drawn to the piano,
but I'm daunted when I play,
I tend to be ungainly,
and my ears get in the way.

My trunk is far too powerful,
no sooner do I sneeze
than windows crack and shatter
from the impact of the breeze.
I'm plagued by a peculiar,
purely pachydermal plight—
I find no socks and underwear
that fit precisely right.

Rat for Lunch!

Rat for lunch! Rat for lunch!
Yum! Delicious! Munch munch munch!
One by one or by the bunch—
Rat, oh rat, oh rat for lunch!

Scrambled slug in salty slime
is our choice at breakfast time,
but for lunch, we say to you,
nothing but a rat will do.

Rat for lunch! Rat for lunch!
Yum! Delicious! Munch munch munch!
One by one or by the bunch—
Rat, oh rat, oh rat for lunch!

For our snack each afternoon,
we chew bits of baked baboon,
curried squirrel, buttered bat,
but for lunch it must be rat.

Rat for lunch! Rat for lunch!
Yum! Delicious! Munch munch munch!
One by one or by the bunch—
Rat, oh rat, oh rat for lunch!

In the evening we may dine
on fillet of porcupine,
buzzard gizzard, lizard chops,
but for lunch a rat is tops.

Rat for lunch! Rat for lunch!
Yum! Delicious! Munch munch munch!
One by one or by the bunch—
Rat, oh rat, oh rat for lunch!

Rat, we love you steamed or stewed,
blackened, broiled, or barbecued.
Pickled, poached, or fried in fat,
there is nothing like a rat.

Rat for lunch! Rat for lunch!
Yum! Delicious! Munch munch munch!
One by one or by the bunch—
Rat, oh rat, oh rat for lunch!

I Wear the Most Amazing Shoes

I wear the most amazing shoes
the world has ever seen.
The left is pink and purple,
and the right is gold and green.
They have ribbons, beads, and spangles,
buckles, bangles, belts, and bows,
and assorted silver sequins
that illuminate the toes.

They have multicolored laces,
flashing blinkers on the heels.
They have beepers, bells, and buzzers,
and a strange device that squeals.
It only takes an hour a day
to keep them looking clean—
the most amazing pair of shoes
the world has ever seen.

Chuck

I'm Chuck, the chore evader
and adept procrastinator.
I've got a lot of strategies—
I'll demonstrate them later.

I Like the Floppy Dog Downstairs

I like the floppy dog downstairs,
its temperament is sweet.
We often chase each other,
playing tag along the street.

I like the fuzzy dog next door
that knows a lot of tricks.
It wags its tail, it licks my face,
then runs and fetches sticks.

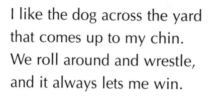

I like the dog across the yard
that comes up to my chin.
We roll around and wrestle,
and it always lets me win.

There is one dog I do not like,
it doesn't growl or bite.
It simply sleeps and sleeps all day,
then barks and barks all night.

Reverso Is Name My

Reverso is name my,
way this talk often I,
say you of many so,
"you follow don't we, No!"

Style my by puzzled you're,
shout you would else why for,
"noise that stop, quiet Be,
much it like not do we!"

Clear rather it's me to,
learn to wish not do you,
you for feel I sad how—
away go will I now.

The Fummawummalummazumms

The Fummawummalummazumms
are zooming through my room,
they are zooming zooming zooming forth and back.
they are humming, they are strumming,
they are thrumming as they zoom,
in their Fummawummalummazumm attack.

Those Fummawummalummazumms
are gumming up my brains
with their zigzag zooming thrumming strumming hums.
And I cannot hope to slumber
while a single one remains,
I'm undone by Fummawummalummazumms.

I have opened all my windows,
though I surely should have known
that those Fummawummalummazumms are smart.
They have summoned some companions,
so their numbers now have grown,
I'm unable to compel them to depart.

I'm succumbing to those numbing
Fummawummalummazumms,
they are humming strumming thrumming on and on.
Now they're drumming as they're humming . . .
I can't wait till morning comes,
and those Fummawummalummazumms are gone.

When I Am Full of Silence

When I am full of silence,
and no one else is near,
the voice I keep inside of me
is all I want to hear.
I settle in my secret place,
contented and alone,
and think no other thoughts except
the thoughts that are my own.

When I am full of silence,
I do not care to play,
to run and jump and fuss about,
the way I do all day.
The pictures painted in my mind
are all I need to see
when I am full of silence . . .
when I am truly me.

A Puzzled Python

A puzzled python shook its head
and said, "I simply fail
to tell if I am purely neck,
or else entirely tail."

Owlsong

If I were as wise
as many have said,
I wouldn't eat mice,
I'd be in my bed.

I'm not in my bed,
I'm prowling the skies,
so mice be aware . . .
I'm not all that wise.

A Dizzy Little Duzzle

I'M A DIZZY LITTLE DUZZLE AND I DO THE BEST I CAN AS I AIMLESSLY MEANDER WITH NO PURPOSE AND NO PLAN • THOUGH I'M BUT A DIZZY DUZZLE WHERE I BEGAN AND MY FINAL DESTINATION IS OF SIMPLY NO CONCERN YET I ALWAYS SEEM TO MANAGE TO ARRIVE AT A SINGLE PLACE I'VE BEEN FOR A WHILE I MAY GO STRAIGHTER THAN A TRAIN UPON A TRACK THEN FOR NO APPARENT REASON CHANGE MY COURSE AND DOUBLE BACK MY APPROACH IS SO HAPHAZARD I AM BOUND TO LOSE MY WAY AS MY RANDOM TRANSMIGRATION TAKES ME HOPELESSLY ASTRAY I MAY AMBLE IN A CIRCLE MAKE AN UNEXPECTED TURN AND MY FINAL DESTINATION IS OF PURPOSE AND NO PLAN I DON'T PAY THE LEAST ATTENTION AS I WANDER OUT AND IN SO I HAVEN'T ANY NOTION OF

My Glider

My glider is graceful,
my glider is grand,
I launch it aloft
with a flick of my hand.
It smoothly ascends,
then it pauses and swoops,
it hovers in space
and turns intricate loops.

My glider is delicate,
nimble and rare,
it rises on gossamer
currents of air.
My glider is presently
useless to me—
my glider is stuck
in a very tall tree.

Raisins

I used to put raisins on oatmeal,
until that indelible day
when one sleepy raisin awakened
and rapidly scampered away.

We're Loudies!

We're **Loudies**, *loud* **Loudies**!
We're *loud*, very *loud*.
Our overblown voices
stand out in a crowd.
We **yell** and we **yammer**,
we **bellow** and **bray**,
too dense to admit
that we've nothing to say.

We're **Loudies**, *loud* **Loudies**!
We never turn off.
We're *louder* than hogs
swilling slop from a trough.
We constantly **crow**.
We incessantly **shout**,
our only intention
is drowning you out.

Our trivial minds
are essentially numb.
We have no ideas,
our opinions are dumb.
We listen to no one,
we don't care to learn,
to shout very **_loud_**
is our only concern.

When **_loud_ Loudies** meet,
we start wagging our tongues.
We open our throats
and we **shout** out our lungs.
We **bluster** and **boast**
until both of us burst—
no **_loud_ Loudie** stops
till the other stops first!

Zeke McPeake

I'm Zeke McPeake,
and when I speak,
my voice is but
a teeny squeak.

No matter how
I try to shout,
I can't make more
than this come out.

If I should whisper,
strain your ears,
the volume almost
disappears.

I'm Zeke McPeake,
I talk this way,
so listen close—
I've much to say.

142

I've Got a Three-Thousand-Pound Cat

I've got a three-thousand-pound cat
that isn't much help in my house.
The reason is probably that
I've got a four-thousand-pound mouse.

We Often Walk on Water

We often walk on water,
and as we do, we think
that we've no explanation
for why we never sink.
Though we're not very heavy,
we're also not that light.
Our weight is more than adequate
for us to slip from sight.

We go out every morning
and stroll upon a lake,
attracting flocks of waterfowl
who follow in our wake.
Astonished at our presence,
they cannot help but quack.
We wave in recognition
and quack directly back.

We step there as securely
as *you* step on a street,
remaining dry, unless you count
the bottoms of our feet.
We find the lake as solid
as a sidewalk or a floor.
We often walk on water—
we sometimes sink on shore!

I Hide My Dromedary

I hide my dromedary
inside of our garage,
my parents don't suspect it's there . . .
it's wearing camel-flage.

When Daddy Sat on the Tomatoes

When Daddy sat on the tomatoes
that *somebody* put on his chair,
he shot from that seat like a rocket
and practically flew through the air.
I thought he would go through the ceiling.
"Who did that! Who did that!" he roared.
If there were awards for conniptions,
then he would have won an award.

He ranted all over the kitchen
and did a ridiculous dance.
He really was something to look at,
tomato all over his pants.
He raved like a ruffled old rooster,
he growled like a furious bear,
the time he sat on the tomatoes
that *somebody* put on his chair.

Sad Little Duck Song

I'm feeling down today,
I cannot pay my bill.
I don't believe the pelican,
and doubt the whippoorwill.

Grandpa McWheeze

I'm Grandpa McWheeze,
and I do as I please,
I'm quite a remarkable fellow.
I stand on my head
while I butter my bread,
or paint my rhinoceros yellow.

I'm building a boat
I've designed not to float,
I frequently read in the shower.
I play two bassoons
that I fashioned from prunes,
I tango in barrels of flour.

I'm Grandpa McWheeze,
I tie springs to my knees,
I live in a hollow old tree.
I wear snakes on my neck,
and I sort of suspect
there are very few grandpas like me.

I'm Proud of My Preposterpus

I'm proud of my Preposterpus,
so ponderous and pale,
I love the way it whistles
when it swizzles ginger ale.
It's magnificent in stature,
fully twenty-four feet tall,
so it tends to draw attention
when I take it to the mall.

It has talons like an eagle,
shiny flippers like a seal,
rows of webbing at its elbows,
and a head of solid steel.
With its pickle-like proboscis,
glossy antlers, rosy beak,
it's apparent my Preposterpus
is practically unique.

My Preposterpus eats peanuts
and potatoes from my hand,
and will juggle ten umbrellas
at my tiniest command.
It whinnies, whines, and warbles,
it has fascinating ways,
it can dance a tarantella
as it gobbles mayonnaise.

There's no other creature like it,
it has feathers, scales, and hair,
so I fancied it would triumph
in the pet show at the fair.
I'm proud of my Preposterpus,
my fish-frog-mammal-bird—
there were forty-four contestants,
and it finished forty-third.

If

If a baseball breaks a window,
does it cause the window pain?
If it rains upon a lion,
do the droplets water mane?
If you try to wring a lemon,
can you hear the lemon peal?
If you dream that you are fishing,
is your dream of fishing real?

If an ogre is unhappy,
does it utter giant sighs?
If you catch a booby snooping,
are you sure the booby pries?
If you bleach a bag of garbage,
do you turn the garbage pale?
If you tell a horse a story,
could it be a pony tale?

If you wish to paint a whistle,
will you make the whistle blue?
If you're stuck inside a chimney,
do you suffer from the flue?
If you sketch an escalator,
did you practice drawing stairs?
If you separate two rabbits,
are you really splitting hares?

If you're filling in a doughnut,
do you make the doughnut whole?
If you're posing as a muffin,
are you acting out a roll?
If your conversation sparkles,
do you thank your diamond mind?
If you're followed by a grizzly,
do you have a bear behind?

Index to Titles

Index to First Lines